Indiana

A Buddy Book
by

Julie Murray

ABDO
Publishing Company

VISIT US AT
www.abdopub.com

Published by ABDO Publishing Company, 4940 Viking Drive, Edina, Minnesota 55435.

Copyright © 2006 by Abdo Consulting Group, Inc. International copyrights reserved in all countries. No part of this book may be reproduced in any form without written permission from the publisher. Buddy Books™ is a trademark and logo of ABDO Publishing Company.

Printed in the United States.

Edited by: Sarah Tieck
Contributing Editor: Michael P. Goecke
Graphic Design: Deb Coldiron, Maria Hosley
Image Research: Sarah Tieck
Photographs: Brand X Pictures, City of Fort Wayne, Clipart.com, Eyewire, Getty Images, Library of Congress, Medio Images, One Mile Up, PhotoDisc

Library of Congress Cataloging-in-Publication Data

Murray, Julie, 1969-
 Indiana / Julie Murray.
  p. cm. — (The United States)
 Includes bibliographical references (p.) and index.
 ISBN 1-59197-673-1
  1. Indiana—Juvenile literature. I. Title.

F526.3.M87 2005
977.2—dc22

2004058098

Table Of Contents

A Snapshot Of Indiana

Indiana is known for its landscape. There are low hills made up of sand and rocks, sandy dunes, lakes and marshes, and the Midwestern Corn Belt's rich soil to name a few.

There are 50 states in the United States. Every state is different. Every state has an official state nickname. Indiana is sometimes called the "Hoosier State." No one knows exactly why. Some people think the name comes from a man named Sam Hoosier. He was a builder.

Farmers in Indiana grow marigolds.

Indiana became the 19th state on December 11, 1816. Today, Indiana is the 38th-largest state in the United States. It covers 36,185 square miles (93,719 sq km). It is home to 6,080,485 people.

Where Is Indiana?

There are four parts of the United States. Each part is called a region. Each region is in a different area of the country. The United States Census Bureau says the four regions are the Northeast, the South, the Midwest, and the West.

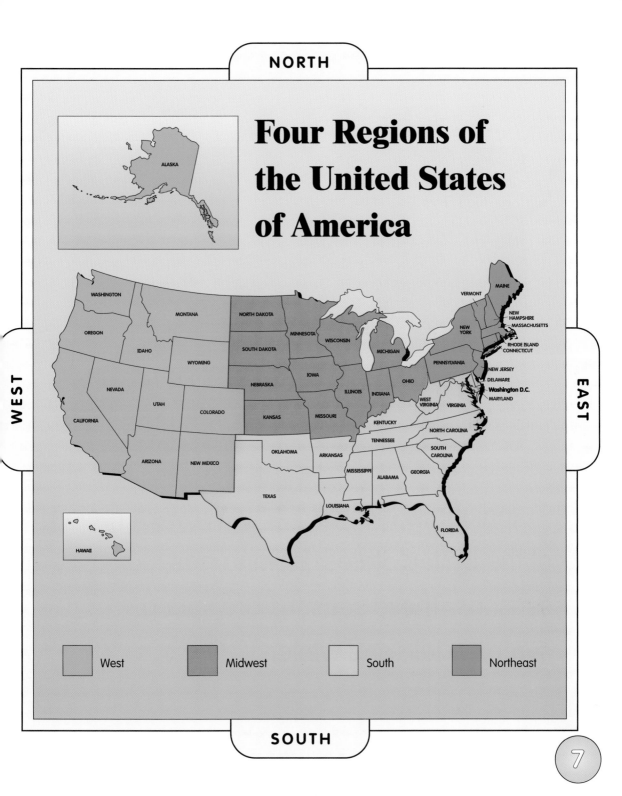

Four Regions of the United States of America

ALASKA

WASHINGTON

MONTANA

NORTH DAKOTA

VERMONT

MAINE

OREGON

IDAHO

WYOMING

SOUTH DAKOTA

MINNESOTA

WISCONSIN

MICHIGAN

NEW YORK

NEW HAMPSHIRE

MASSACHUSETTS

RHODE ISLAND

CONNECTICUT

NEVADA

UTAH

COLORADO

NEBRASKA

IOWA

ILLINOIS

INDIANA

OHIO

PENNSYLVANIA

NEW JERSEY

DELAWARE

Washington D.C.

MARYLAND

CALIFORNIA

ARIZONA

NEW MEXICO

KANSAS

MISSOURI

KENTUCKY

WEST VIRGINIA

VIRGINIA

NORTH CAROLINA

OKLAHOMA

ARKANSAS

TENNESSEE

SOUTH CAROLINA

TEXAS

MISSISSIPPI

ALABAMA

GEORGIA

LOUISIANA

FLORIDA

HAWAII

West   Midwest   South   Northeast

Indiana's weather is warm in the summer months.

Indiana is located in the Midwest region of the United States. Indiana has four seasons. These seasons are spring, summer, fall, and winter.

Indiana is the smallest state in the Midwest. It is bordered by four other states. Michigan lies to the north. Ohio is to the east. Kentucky is to the south. Illinois is to the west. Lake Michigan makes up the border on the northwest corner of the state.

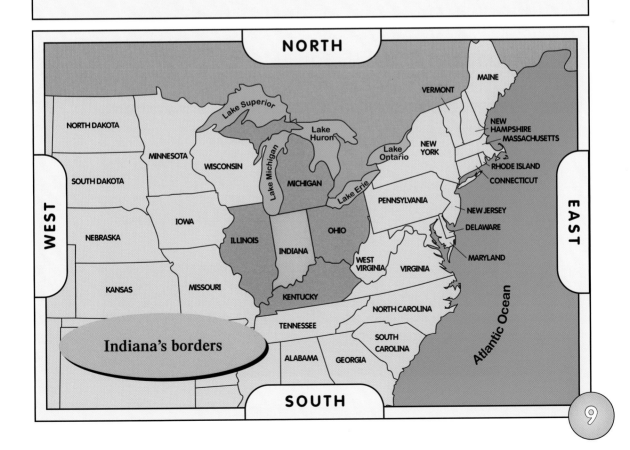

Indiana's borders

Indiana

State abbreviation: IN

State nickname: The Hoosier State

State capital: Indianapolis

State motto: The Crossroads of America

Statehood: December 11, 1816, 19th state

Population: 6,080,485, ranks 14th

State flag:
Adopted in 1917

Land area: 36,185 square miles (93,719 sq km), ranks 38th

State song: "On the Banks of the Wabash, Far Away"

State government: Three branches: legislative, executive, and judicial

Average July temperature: 75°F (24°C)

Average January temperature: 28°F (-2°C)

State flower: Peony

State tree: Tulip poplar

State bird: Cardinal

Cities And The Capital

The capital of Indiana is Indianapolis. It is also the largest city in the state. Indianapolis is famous for auto racing. The Indianapolis Motor Speedway is home to the Indy 500. It is a famous auto race. Thousands of people come to Indianapolis every Memorial Day weekend to see the top racers from around the world compete.

Indiana's capitol building is in Indianapolis.

On oval tracks, Indy race cars can go
more than 200 miles (322 km) per hour.

The skyline of Fort Wayne.

Fort Wayne is the second-largest city in Indiana. This city is located where three rivers come together. These rivers are the Maumee, the St. Marys, and the St. Joseph rivers.

Famous Citizens

Wilbur Wright (1867–1912)

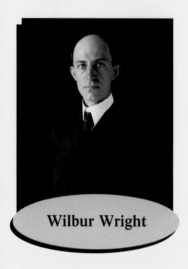

Wilbur Wright

Wilbur Wright was born in 1867 in New Castle. He and his brother, Orville Wright, are famous. Together, they invented the first flying machine that actually flew. Their airplane flew for the first time near Kitty Hawk, North Carolina. This happened on December 17, 1903. Wilbur is known for the longest flight on this day. He flew 852 feet (260 m) in about one minute.

Wibur Wright flying his airplane.

Famous Citizens

Larry Bird (1956–)

Larry Bird was born in French Lick in 1956. He is one of the greatest basketball players ever to play the game. He is known for having skills in all areas. He played for Indiana State University from 1975 to 1979. After that, he played for the Boston Celtics from 1979 to 1992. Today, he works with the Indiana Pacers.

Larry Bird

Indiana Limestone

Limestone is rock. It is made from a mineral called calcite. Usually limestone is gray. But, it can be many different colors. Large amounts of limestone are found in the southern part of Indiana.

The United States Treasury is made from Indiana limestone.

Some people say Indiana limestone is the best in the world. Indiana's quarries provide about half of the United States limestone. This is used to build many famous buildings. Some of these buildings include the Empire State Building, the Pentagon, and the United States Treasury.

The Amish

Indiana is one of five states in the United States with a large community of Amish people. Most of the Amish people in Indiana live in the northeastern part of the state.

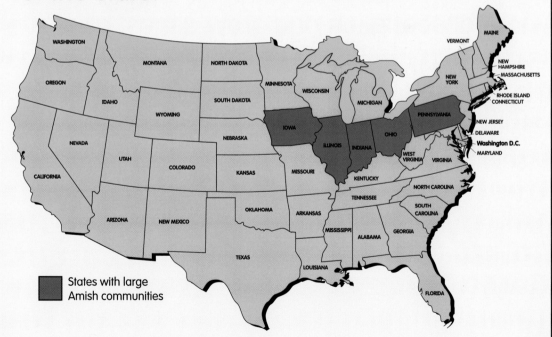

States with large Amish communities

The Amish are a group of people who believe in living a simple life free of modern things. This means they do not have cars or televisions. They use horses and buggies for transportation and grow almost all of the food they eat on their farms. The men and women dress in plain clothes that are sewn by the women.

The Amish people don't drive cars.

The Amish are known for their great woodworking. People can buy Amish-made furniture in many places around the United States.

Indiana Dunes

Indiana Dunes National Lakeshore is known for its sand dunes. It is also known for its many unique native plants. Ninety of these plant species are threatened, or endangered.

Indiana Dunes State Park is part of Indiana Dunes National Lakeshore. Visitors to the state park can walk among 200-foot (61-m) high sand dunes. Sand dunes are mounds of sand created by the wind. Over thousands of years, water and wind have formed the dunes. The dunes continue to change every day.

Indiana Dunes National Lakeshore has many rare flowers and plants.

People hike and have picnics on
the beaches, dunes, and forests.

Indiana Dunes State Park sits on 2,182 acres (883 ha) of land. The dunes rise off the shore of Lake Michigan. The park is along three miles (five km) of the shores of Lake Michigan. Lake Michigan is the third-largest of the five Great Lakes.

In Indiana Dunes State Park, people hike through the great dunes, beaches, and forests. They also camp and learn about the dunes.

Indiana

1679: French explorer Robert Cavelier arrives in Indiana.

1811: General William Henry Harrison and his army defeat many Native American tribes in the Battle of Tippecanoe.

1816: On December 11, Indiana becomes the 19th state.

William Henry Harrison

1841: William Henry Harrison, former governor of the Indiana Territory, becomes president of the United States in March. He dies 30 days later.

1871: The Fort Wayne Kekiongas play the Cleveland Forest Citys on May 4. This is the first professional baseball game.

1889: Standard Oil Company builds an oil refinery in Whiting. It is one of the world's largest oil refineries.

1894: Elwood Haynes invents the first gasoline-powered car. He does this in Kokomo.

1911: The first Indy 500 race takes place at the Indianapolis Motor Speedway.

1914: A cartoonist named Johnny Gruelle creates the Raggedy Ann doll for his daughter Marcella Gruelle.

1937: The Ohio River overflows, creating a flood in Evansville and other river cities in southern Indiana.

1963: The Studebaker Corporation stops making cars in South Bend after 59 years of production.

1989: Dan Quayle of Indianapolis becomes vice president of the United States.

2004: Peyton Manning of the Indianapolis Colts breaks an NFL record on December 26 with 49 touchdown passes in one season.

Dan Quayle

Cities in Indiana

Whiting

South Bend

Fort Wayne ●

● Kokomo

Indianapolis ★

● New Castle

French Lick ●

Important Words

American Civil War the United States war between the Northern and the Southern states.

capital a city where government leaders meet.

endangered in danger of dying out.

modern the way of life in the present time.

nickname a name that describes something special about a person or a place.

slavery the owning of people as slaves.

unique being the only one of its kind.

Web Sites

To learn more about Indiana, visit ABDO Publishing Company on the World Wide Web. Web site links about Indiana are featured on our Book Links page. These links are routinely monitored and updated to provide the most current information available.

www.abdopub.com

Index